Our Grandparents Were Members of the Black Panther Party

By: Fatima D. El-Mekki

Edited by: Khalid and Dr. Angela Crumdy

“Zakiyyah, what do you think readers of our age range (seven to ten years old) would say if we told them our grandparents were Black Panthers?” Zaynab asked her little sister.

“I am sure they will think of Wakanda. You know that fictional country in Africa that has T’Chala as a king, and he transforms into a Black Panther when he fights? He has a sister who is very smart. Maybe they would think that our grandparents played a role in the movie?” answered Zakiyyah still wondering.

“But Zaynab, since that is not the case, I think it will be a good opportunity to share what being a Black Panther meant at the time of our grandparents!” said Zakiyyah excitedly.

“That’s a great idea! We can just tell the readers what our grandparents told us and everything we know about them. It is easy to do!” added Zaynab.

“First, let’s talk about the Black Panther Party (BPP) and then about our grandparents.”

The Black Panther Party was created in Oakland, California, in October 1966 by Huey P. Newton and Bobby Seale. It was dissolved in 1982.

As you can guess by its name, the emblem was a black panther like the one on our scarves.

The choice of this animal, as explained by the co-founder Huey P. Newton, was because it is not in the panther's nature to attack anyone first. He responds when he is attacked and backed into a corner.

The Panthers were reacting to an action that was made against African Americans, which was oppression. They were attacked; therefore, they responded.

They loved the people, and their motto was "Love for the People," which meant that in order to be a revolutionary, you had to love the people.

The members used to wear black berets, black leather jackets, and had a natural hairstyle called an "Afro."

Because of the love the Black Panthers had for the people, they would hold meetings in the community to listen to them. During these meetings, the people would tell the Panthers their needs and complaints. The Panthers would establish programs based on the people's needs, such as the Free Breakfast, clothing and medical programs.

One of the goals of the BPP was to fight against police brutality as many Black people were killed by police.

So, the Party wanted to be the police of the police because enough was enough.

Besides fighting against police brutality, the Black Panther Party fought for economic and political equality, representation, free education, free health care, and free food programs.

The Black Panthers wanted to help African Americans in poverty to have a better life; they wanted to help the community.

Through them, the disease called sickle cell anemia, which affects mostly Black people, was finally screened for nationwide. It is a painful and deadly disease. Because the BPP advocated so hard, President Nixon signed legislation to work hard to find a cure in order to help those who have the disease.

The free education program was important because they wanted African Americans to have access to an education system that teaches them knowledge about themselves, because you know, we should tell our own history.

The Free Breakfast for School Children Program was, as understood by its name, to give food for free. Getting free food at school was a program that the Black Panthers started. Before them, nobody else has done it consistently. We like that program because we think that it is important to eat and have energy to study. It is very hard to focus when you are hungry. Every child deserves food! And, because of the BPP, that program still exists in today's schools.

Power to the People!

It was a slogan used by the Black Panthers to fight oppression with the fist up.

When your fingers make a fist, it is hard to divide the hand. That's one of the reasons you will see Black Panther putting their fists like that. It represents unity with people who are oppressed. If we are together, nothing will separate us, and we will be strong.

Unfortunately, many years after the Party was dissolved, Black and Brown people are still being killed and oppressed. Is it because we are not strongly united? What do you think?

Violence has never been a good thing, neither has oppression, injustice, or discrimination.

“Did the Black Panthers have allies?” asked Zakiyyah.

Yes, one example is the White Panthers. Once, Huey P. Newton, co-founder of the BPP was asked how white people could help the Party. He said that they could create the White Panther Party. It was founded in 1968 by Pun Plamondon, Leni Sinclair, and John Sinclair. They were striving to be anti-racists.

“Do you remember taking this picture dressed like Angela Davis during Black History month?” Mommy made a collage of Zakiyyah’s picture and Davis’s. Angela Davis was supporting the cause of the Black Panther Party, and still today, she is a voice against oppression and injustice.

Now, let's talk about our grandmother.

We affectionately called our grandmother "Bibi." She was born Saundra Dickerson. She changed her name to Aisha El-Mekki when she became a Muslim. Born in Philadelphia on April 21, 1947, she used to attend a Catholic school. When she became a teenager, she used to listen to records with her Aunt Maryam El-Mekki Abdullah; mostly speeches given by Malcolm X.

She loved Malcolm X so much. She would teach us about him. She had a picture of him in the foyer and a large poster on the door of a room in her house.

She never liked oppression and always wanted to stand against injustice, which led her on a long journey into learning how to fight against it.

When she heard about the Black Panther Party and the food program they had, she found it marvelous that an organization would feed the Black children every day and for free! She did more research about the Black Panther Party and decided to join them so she could make her contribution to supporting Black children. She used to help at the Free Breakfast (for school) and clothing (children) programs. She was assigned to the West Philly branch but would also work at the North Philly office.

A few months after joining the Black Panther Party, she met our grandfather, and they got married. Because they were both members of the BPP, life wasn't easy for them. Life is never easy for heroes who fight for justice. After giving birth to our dad and our uncle, they had to go their separate ways because of political tension, and constant threats of violence by the police and the FBI.

Bibi was happy when we could go to protest with her. She wanted to make it clear that the fight for justice was for women of all ages. Therefore, we had to be introduced to organizing and activism within the community at an early age.

Every first Sunday of the month, we used to have family brunch with her, and she wanted to make sure that we knew the Black National Anthem, "Lift Every Voice and Sing." She loved singing it!

Ok, we should admit that we don't know all the words yet, but we are working on it. That anthem is important for us as African Americans because through it we pledge unity, we learn history lessons, and we get together to fight injustice.

Now that she is no longer with us, because she has transitioned and joined the ancestors, our parents take us to meetings or book signings such as Comrade Sisters: Women of the Black Panther Party by Stephen Shames and Ericka Huggins. Sometimes we meet other Black Panther Party members who share their stories. Although we are too young to understand everything, it is important to attend the programs and learn what we can about our history.

Look at this beautiful mural!

It is in West Oakland, California.

The mural honors the women of the Black Panther Party. The name of our grandmother and many other women are written on it. Our dad took the picture when he went to Oakland. We haven't had the chance to visit the place yet, but we hope we will. If you go before us, check for our grandmother's name. Do you think you will remember?

We will always remember Bibi as a loving grandmother, who loved to read us books and send us cards on different occasions.

She used to say, "Justice will give birth to peace." It is forever marked in our memories, and it should lead us on our path and strengthen our determination.

Now, it is time to talk about our grandfather Khalid, who we call "Abu" or "Pop-Pop."

In this picture taken by Stephen Shames, our grandfather was holding a Black Panther Party newspaper. He became a Panther when he was about 17 years old. He was known as Dante in the Party. He said that there was one important condition that was required before joining the BPP, it was to know how to read.

When he joined the Black Panther Party, he started by selling the Black Panther newspapers. It used to publish the Party's activities, ideology, and the struggles of African Americans all over the world. It was sold at 25 cents at the time.

Everyone at one time or another was required to sell the papers and sometimes Panthers would give the newspapers away for free because it was important to get the information to the people.

Pop-Pop was assigned to the West Philly branch where he was in charge of security. In 1970, Black Panther Party members were handcuffed, stripped and forced by the police to line up against the wall of a building at gunpoint.

In this picture, you can have a better understanding of what happened. Pop-Pop is the third person from the right.

Our grandfather makes sure that we understand the struggles African Americans and oppressed people around the world are facing. We have a lot to learn from his experience.

There is something we loved doing since we were small, and that is to play with our grandfather's beard and hair. Gardening is also something we do with him because it is one of his favorite activities. He teaches us a lot about trees, flowers, insects, as well as other creatures. During those moments, he would talk to us about love for human beings and how it's important to treat even an ant with kindness.

Even though our grandparents were no longer married, they kept a good relationship full of respect for each other. Sometimes, they used to go to programs together where they would talk about their experiences as Black Panther members.

Children of Black Panther Party Members are called *Cubs* and they grandchildren are called *grand Cubs*.

Our father is a Black Panther Cub.

We are Black Panther grand Cubs.

"Zaynab, since we are Black Panther grand Cubs, do you think that someone who doesn't have parents or grandparents who were Black Panther, can become a Cub? Is it only for us?"

"That's a great question Zakiyyah. You see, the Black Panther Party doesn't formally exist anymore, so no one can become a member nowadays. Therefore, only children of former members can be Cubs. However, the National Alumni Association of the Black Panther Party and their Cubs and grand Cubs are still very active."

"I am so happy that we were able to share the story of our grandparents," said Zakiyyah with a big smile.

We are proud of our grandparents who have shown us the right path. We should never keep quiet when justice is needed. We will make them proud of us, and we will keep their spirit alive.

Do you know if your grandparents or parents were also Black Panther members? If yes, what have they shared with you? Would you like to share it with us; just like we did in a book? We would love to read your family's story.

And remember, we should tell our own history.

"AND THAT IS WHY...THE YOUTH WERE SO IMPORTANT, FOR THEY WOULD PROVE TO THE ANCESTORS THAT IT HAD NOT BEEN FOOLISH TO FIGHT FOR THE RIGHT TO BE FREE, TO BE HUMAN."

Toni Cade Bambara

Made in the USA
Middletown, DE
24 October 2023